Bella Blew
Blue Bubbles

Amanda Rondeau

JACKSON COUNTY LIBRARY SERVICES
MEDFORD, OREGON 97501

Published by SandCastle™, an imprint of ABDO Publishing Company, 4940 Viking Drive, Edina, Minnesota 55435.

Cover and interior photo credits: Digital Vision, Eyewire Images, PhotoDisc,
   Rubberball Productions

Library of Congress Cataloging-in-Publication Data

Rondeau, Amanda, 1974-
   Bella blew blue bubbles / Amanda Rondeau.
      p. cm. -- (Homophones)
   Includes index.
   Summary: Photographs and simple text introduce homophones, words that sound alike but are spelled differently and have different meanings.
   ISBN 1-57765-784-5
   1. English language--Homonyms--Juvenile literature. [1. English language--Homonyms.]
I. Title. II. Series.

PE1595 .R66 2002
428.1--dc21
                                                                    2001053374

The SandCastle concept, content, and reading method have been reviewed and approved by a national advisory board including literacy specialists, librarians, elementary school teachers, early childhood education professionals, and parents.

Let Us Know

After reading the book, SandCastle would like you to tell us your stories about reading. What is your favorite page? Was there something hard that you needed help with? Share the ups and downs of learning to read. We want to hear from you! To get posted on the ABDO Publishing Company Web site, send us email at:

sandcastle@abdopub.com

About SandCastle™
Nonfiction books for the beginning reader

- Basic concepts of phonics are incorporated with integrated language methods of reading instruction. Most words are short, and phrases, letter sounds, and word sounds are repeated.

- Book levels are based on the ATOS™ for Books formula. Other considerations for readability include the number of words in each sentence, the number of characters in each word, and word lists based on curriculum frameworks.

- Full-color photography reinforces word meanings and concepts.

- "Words I Can Read" list at the end of each book teaches basic elements of grammar, helps the reader recognize the words in the text, and builds vocabulary.

- Reading levels are indicated by the number of flags on the castle.

SandCastle uses the following definitions for this series:

- Homographs: words that are spelled the same but sound different and have different meanings. *Easy memory tip: "-graph"= same look*

- Homonyms: words that are spelled and sound the same but have different meanings. *Easy memory tip: "-nym"= same name*

- Homophones: words that sound alike but are spelled differently and have different meanings. *Easy memory tip: "-phone"= sound alike*

Look for more SandCastle books in these three reading levels:

Level 1 (one flag)	**Level 2** (two flags)	**Level 3** (three flags)

Grades Pre-K to K 5 or fewer words per page	**Grades K to 1** 5 to 10 words per page	**Grades 1 to 2** 10 to 15 words per page

Note: Some pages in this book contain more than 10 words in order to more clearly convey the concept of the book.

bass

base

Homophones are words that sound alike but are spelled differently and have different meanings.

The big brown bear caught
a fish.

Matt is not wearing a shirt.

His back is bare.

Martha removes nails from a board.

Amalia is bored.

She wants to play.

Aki took a bow at the end
of the dance.

Two raccoons sit on the
bough of a tree.

We like to build sand castles.

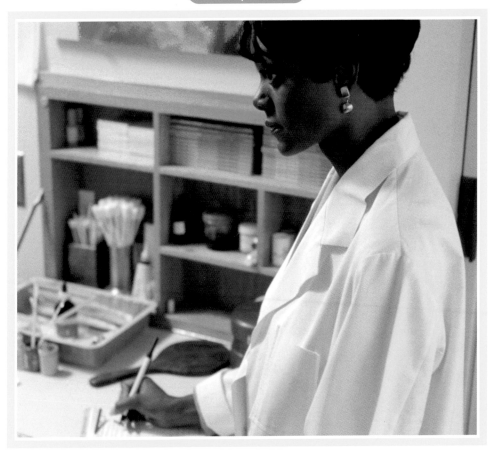

The doctor billed us for
the visit.

Bill and Brian take a break.

Dad is teaching Jill to brake.

Sofia beats the eggs for
a cake.

Beets are red and grow underground.

Jan buries the roots of the plant in dirt.

These berries are covered in snow.

Lauren is wearing a
bridal gown.

What kind of animal wears a bridle?

(horse)

Words I Can Read

Nouns

A noun is a person, place, or thing

animal (AN-uh-muhl) p. 21
back (BAK) p. 7
base (BAYSS) p. 4
bass (BAYSS) p. 4
bear (BAIR) p. 6
board (BORD) p. 8
bough (BOU) p. 11
bow (BOU) p. 10
break (BRAYK) p. 14

bridle (BRYE-duhl) p. 21
cake (KAYK) p. 16
dance (DANSS) p. 10
dirt (DURT) p. 18
doctor (DOK-tur) p. 13
end (END) p. 10
fish (FISH) p. 6
gown (GOUN) p. 20

horse (HORSS) p. 21
kind (KINDE) p. 21
plant (PLANT) p. 18
sand castle (SAND KASS-uhl) p. 12
shirt (SHURT) p. 7
snow (SNOH) p. 19
tree (TREE) p. 11
visit (VIZ-it) p. 13

Plural Nouns

A plural noun is more than one person, place, or thing

beets (BEETSS) p. 17
berries (BER-eez) p. 19
castles (KASS-uhlz) p. 12

eggs (EGZ) p. 16
homophones (HOME-uh-fonez) p. 5
meanings (MEE-ningz) p. 5

nails (NAYLZ) p. 8
raccoons (ra-KOONZ) p. 11
roots (ROOTSS) p. 18
words (WURDZ) p. 5

Proper Nouns
A proper noun is the name of a person, place, or thing

Aki (AH-kee) p. 10
Amalia
  (uh-MAH-lee-uh)
  p. 9
Bill (BIL) p. 14

Brian (BRYE-uhn) p. 14
Dad (DAD) p. 15
Jan (JAN) p. 18
Jill (JIL) p. 15
Lauren (LOR-en) p. 20

Martha (MAR-thuh)
  p. 8
Matt (MAT) p. 7
Sofia (soh-FEE-uh)
  p. 16

Verbs
A verb is an action or being word

are (AR) pp. 5, 17, 19
beats (BEETSS) p. 16
billed (BILD) p. 13
bored (BORD) p. 9
brake (BRAYK) p. 15
build (BILD) p. 12
buries (BER-eez) p. 18
caught (KAWT) p. 6
covered (KUHV-urd)
  p. 19

grow (GROH) p. 17
have (HAV) p. 5
is (IZ) pp. 7, 9, 15, 20
like (LIKE) p. 12
play (PLAY) p. 9
removes
  (ri-MOOVZ) p. 8
sit (SIT) p. 11
sound (SOUND) p. 5
spelled (SPELD) p. 5

take (TAYK) p. 14
teaching (TEECH-ing)
  p. 15
took (TUK) p. 10
wants (WONTSS)
  p. 9
wearing (WAIR-ing)
  pp. 7, 20
wears (WAIRZ) p. 21

Adjectives
An adjective describes something

alike (uh-LIKE) p. 5
bare (BAIR) p. 7
big (BIG) p. 6
bridal (BRYE-duhl)
  p. 20

brown (BROUN) p. 6
different
  (DIF-ur-uhnt) p. 5
his (HIZ) p. 7

red (RED) p. 17
these (THEEZ) p. 19
two (TOO) p. 11

Match these homophones
to the pictures

bare
bear

berries
buries

bough
bow

bridal
bridle